How to Draw
Wild Animals

Christine Smith

For a free color catalog describing Gareth Stevens' list
of high-quality books and multimedia programs,
call 1-800-542-2595 (USA) or 1-800-461-9120 (Canada).
Gareth Stevens Publishing's Fax: (414) 225-0377.
See our catalog, too, on the World Wide Web: http://gsinc.com

Library of Congress Cataloging-in-Publication Data

Smith, Christine (Christine Hunnikin)
   How to draw wild animals / by Christine Smith.
      p. cm. --(Art smart)
   Includes index.
   Summary: Step-by-step instructions for drawing nine different
wild animals.
   ISBN 0-8368-1612-9 (library binding)
   1. Wildlife in art--Juvenile literature. 2. Drawing--Technique--
Juvenile literature.   [1. Wildlife in art. 2. Animals in art
3. Drawing--Technique.] I. Title. II. Series.
NC780.S58 1996
743'.6--dc20   95-53866

First published in North America in 1996 by
Gareth Stevens Publishing, 1555 North RiverCenter Drive,
Suite 201, Milwaukee, Wisconsin, 53212, USA.
Original © 1993 by Regency House Publishing Limited
(Troddy Books imprint), The Grange, Grange Yard, London,
England, SE1 3AG. Text and illustrations by Christine Smith.
Additional end matter © 1996 by Gareth Stevens, Inc.

Printed in the United States

1 2 3 4 5 6 7 8 9 99 98 97 96

Gareth Stevens Publishing
MILWAUKEE

Materials

Drawing pencils have letters printed on them to show the firmness of the lead. Pencils with an *H* have very hard lead. Pencils with an *HB* have medium lead. Pencils with a *B* have soft lead. Use an *HB* pencil to draw the outlines in this book. Then use a *B* pencil to complete the drawings.

This type of pencil sharpener works well because it keeps the shavings inside a container.

Once you have drawn the outlines on a piece of paper, place a thinner sheet of paper over them. Then make a clean, finished drawing, leaving out any unnecessary lines.

Use a soft eraser to make any changes you might want. Color your drawings with felt-tip pens, watercolors, crayons, or colored pencils.

Shapes

Before you begin drawing, practice the shapes above. Draw them over and over again. All the drawings in this book are based on these simple shapes.

Color

Mixing colors is fun whether you are using colored pencils or paints. Mix red and yellow to make orange. Mix blue and yellow to make green. Red and blue make purple.

Wild animals often have special markings
and patterns on their coats that make
them hard to see in their environment.
Some baby animals even have
different markings than
the adults. Notice how
this baby boar is spotted
so that it blends in
with the bushes.

Nature programs on television picture
wild animals in their natural
surroundings. Sketch these animals
on paper, and make note of the
special details about them.

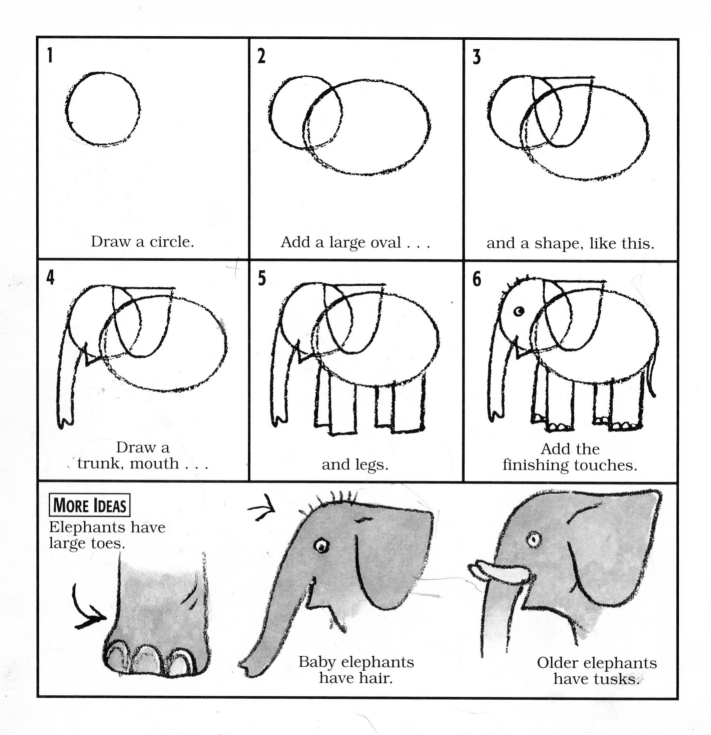

1 Draw a circle.

2 Add a large oval . . .

3 and a shape, like this.

4 Draw a trunk, mouth . . .

5 and legs.

6 Add the finishing touches.

MORE IDEAS

Elephants have large toes.

Baby elephants have hair.

Older elephants have tusks.

Elephant

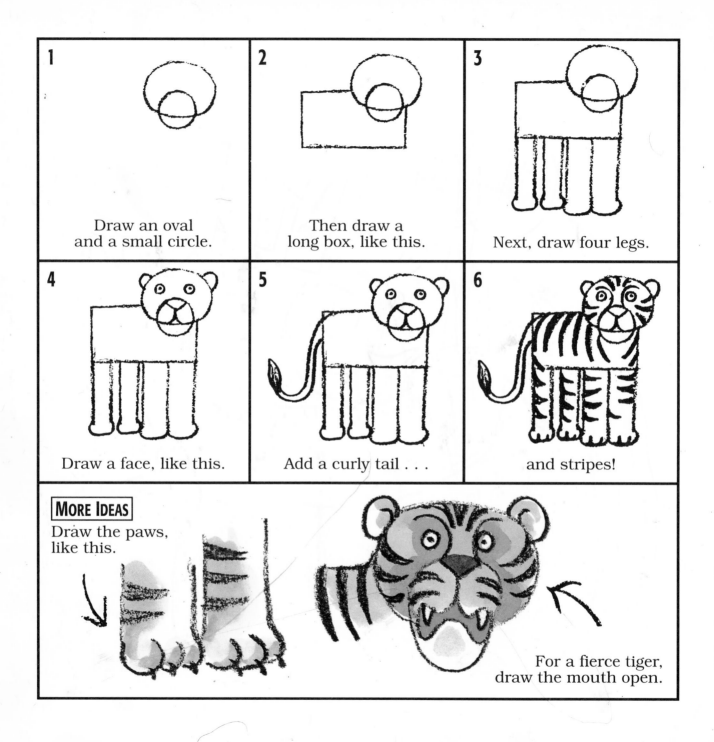

1 Draw an oval and a small circle.

2 Then draw a long box, like this.

3 Next, draw four legs.

4 Draw a face, like this.

5 Add a curly tail . . .

6 and stripes!

MORE IDEAS

Draw the paws, like this.

For a fierce tiger, draw the mouth open.

8

Tiger

1 Draw a long box with a circle inside it.

2 Draw a smaller circle inside and a circle below.

3 Join them like this, and add legs.

4 Double the arm and leg lines, and add a tail.

5 Draw a face, hands, and feet.

6 Draw in lines for hair.

MORE IDEAS

Add details to the face.

Hands and feet can be drawn with more detail, too.

Monkey

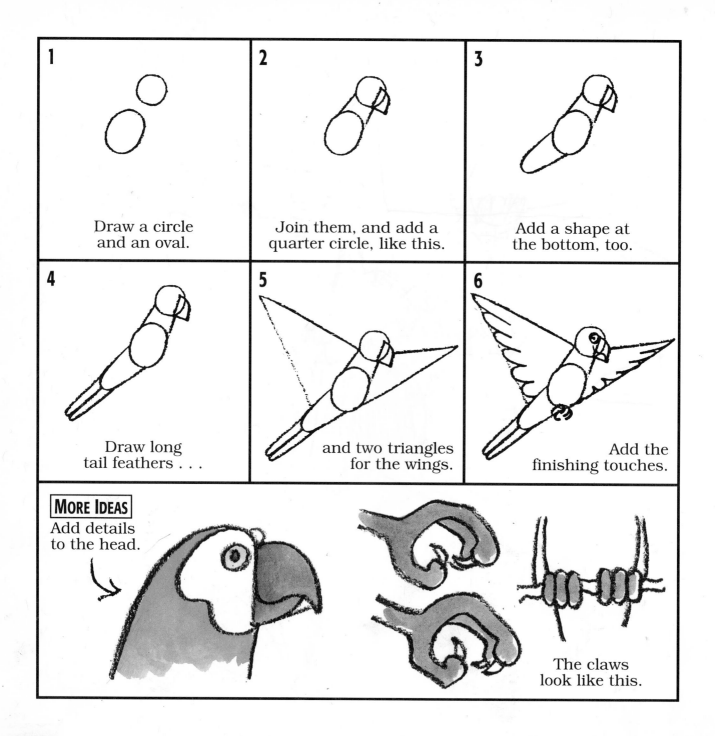

1 Draw a circle and an oval.

2 Join them, and add a quarter circle, like this.

3 Add a shape at the bottom, too.

4 Draw long tail feathers . . .

5 and two triangles for the wings.

6 Add the finishing touches.

MORE IDEAS
Add details to the head.

The claws look like this.

12

Parrot

1 Draw a large oval.

2 Add a smaller oval . . .

3 and another.

4 Draw four legs, like this.

5 Add ears, eyes, and nostrils.

6 Add the finishing touches.

MORE IDEAS

Draw the hippo in water.

Draw a smaller figure for the baby.

14

Hippopotamus

1 Draw a large circle, two smaller circles, and a tiny oval, like this.

2 Join them in this way.

3 Add two leaf shapes for ears.

4 Draw four legs . . .

5 an eye, and a wavy tail.

6 Finish with tusks and a hairy back.

MORE IDEAS
A close-up.

Baby boars have spots. Draw the head like this.

Wild boar

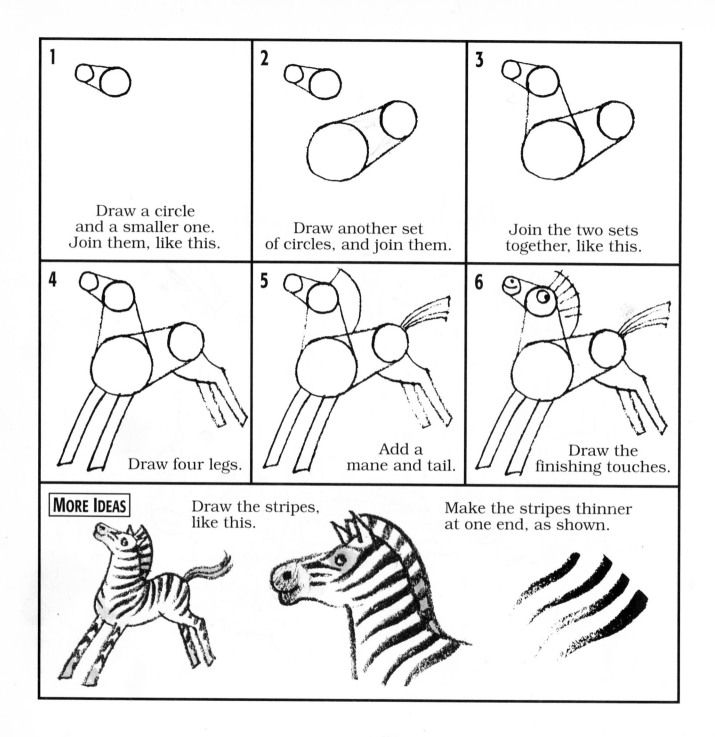

1 Draw a circle and a smaller one. Join them, like this.

2 Draw another set of circles, and join them.

3 Join the two sets together, like this.

4 Draw four legs.

5 Add a mane and tail.

6 Draw the finishing touches.

MORE IDEAS Draw the stripes, like this.

Make the stripes thinner at one end, as shown.

Zebra

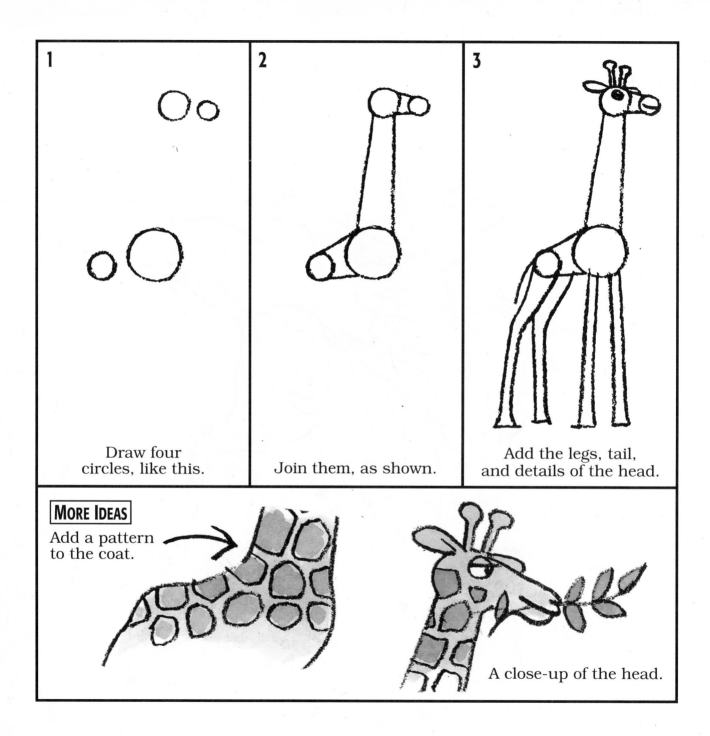

1

Draw four circles, like this.

2

Join them, as shown.

3

Add the legs, tail, and details of the head.

MORE IDEAS

Add a pattern to the coat.

A close-up of the head.

Giraffe

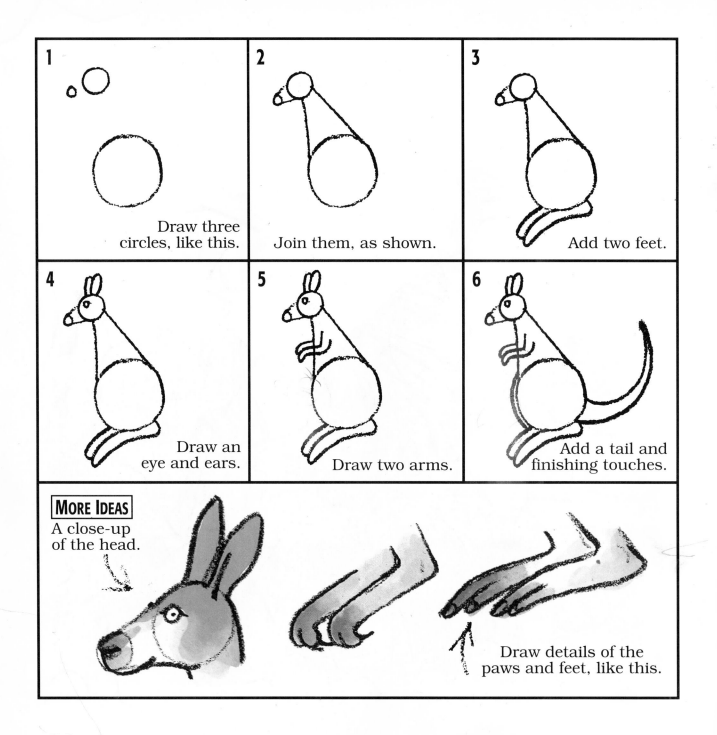

1
Draw three circles, like this.

2
Join them, as shown.

3
Add two feet.

4
Draw an eye and ears.

5
Draw two arms.

6
Add a tail and finishing touches.

MORE IDEAS
A close-up of the head.

Draw details of the paws and feet, like this.

Kangaroo

More Books to Read

African Animals. John W. Purcell (Childrens Press)
Animal Crafts. Worldwide Crafts (series). (Gareth Stevens)
Animal Families (series). (Gareth Stevens)
Animal Wonders (series). (Gareth Stevens)
Animal World (series). Nichols and Schaller (Gareth Stevens)
Animals at a Glance. Wild Animals. (Gareth Stevens)
Draw Animals around the World. Joy Evans (Evan-Moor)
Draw, Model, and Paint (series). (Gareth Stevens)
In Peril (series). Barbara J. Behm and Jean-Christophe Balouet (Gareth Stevens)
Secrets of the Animal World (series). (Gareth Stevens)
Why Are Animals Endangered? Isaac Asimov (Gareth Stevens)

Videos

The Big Cats. Draw Along (series). (Agency for Instructional Technology)
Cougar: King of the Mountain. (Adventure Productions)
Creatures of the Amazon. (Ingram Entertainment)
National Geographic Series: Gorilla, Among the Wild Chimpanzees,
  Really Wild Animals. (Geo Kids)
People of the Forest: The Chimps of Gombe. (Discovery Program)
Zoofari: A Real Life Adventure into the Wilds of the Zoo. (White Tree Pictures)

Index